SOUL CONFESSIONS

**A soul soundtrack of
Schizophrenia: Leona's Lyrics**

*Ancestral Healing: Processing the Past,
Confronting the Present and Healing the Future*

*Confessions of a Daughter as She Reflects on the
Impacts of Mental Illness, Incest, Molestation and
Rape.*

Dedication

This book is dedicated to my mother, Leona Harrison James, my grandmothers', great grandmothers', and aunts'. Women who all suffered in their own pain but still paved the way for me to be greatly inspired to write this book. Your pain and suffering did not go to vain.

Acknowledgment

To my husband

For the tireless nights when it seemed like I was ignoring you, I wasn't. There was a greater good being produced. Thank you for seeing & believing in this vision. Without you there would be no me.

Sensei Subira

For instilling the courage in me to rise like a phoenix from the flames to stand to tell my story

Lynn Monet

My younger self. The scared, timid, confused little girl. Who was born into a world of confusion, who did know where she belonged or how she fit in, who just went along with the flow, who never understood why she was going through what she went through.

I release your anger, pain, sorrow, doubt and fear and I welcome peace, purpose, confidence, creativity, gratitude, and a higher calling of servitude in honor of your transgressions.

Ase'

A Note from the Author

This is the story of a mother's voice. A voice of yells, screams, and shouts for help that fell on deaf ears. A voice that was silenced, and subsequently creating more silenced voices. Silence that perpetrated a choice between a mother, her husband and her child. A choice and a decision that shaped an entire bloodline into fear; depression, bitterness, loneliness, and low self-esteem.

A voice and a choice that became a soundtrack. A soundtrack that gave life & expression to the silenced voice. A soundtrack of music, song, and dance that essentially carried the silenced voice. Until the silenced voice became me, and I became her. This is a story of healing from molestation, rape, and trauma.

The secrets and the deceit to protect ego or to protect a family name, to protect prestige and hold up or to honor a lie. A secret traced through generations, and voiced through this song of spiritual implications.

I am a daughter to a survivor of many forms of sexual abuse including incest, molestation, and rape. Through most of my life, I have lived watching my mother suffer through mental illness as a symptom of her trauma from molestation and rape. Now that I have processed, confronted and learned to heal from my traumas, it has helped me to come to terms with the events that molded most of my life. I am sharing my story to help you avoid the mistakes I've made. I've lived in a plethora of emotions including fear, anger, guilt, low self-esteem, worry, stress, and abandonment. I want to show you how I've overcome my fears and made them my strengths. Turned my pain into power.

The womb carries energy. I was carried in the energy of a womb tainted by sexual trauma. Being conceived and carried in a trauma filled womb has spiritual implications. I marinated in trauma for nine months. I was born into it. It's in my bones, it's in my blood, it's a part of my DNA It became who I was. It was a part of me, and till now, it still is a part of me.

As a result of my mother's condition with bipolar schizophrenia, I grew up watching her take debilitating medications, go through several different therapies, get admitted into several different mental health institutions, and watched her commit several failed suicide attempts. I have lived the life of a survivor and this is my story to all other survivors and their caregivers.

Introduction

My indoctrination into the world of mental health began in the early 1980s. I was about five or six years old at the time. My family and I lived in a two-bedroom duplex home that we owned and rented out the other side. The back of the duplex had a huge wooded backyard.

The neighborhoods back then were very friendly. Everyone knew each other and everyone would often mingle with each other. My friends from the next door and I would go outside and play often, or my mom would host birthday parties and family gatherings in the backyard. It was a warm and a cozy place to grow up.

My mother loved rabbits. We kept them in their cages on the back porch. I think it was their calm and sensual nature that gave her the peace and serenity whenever she would caress them. It was common to find her outside on the back-porch nurturing or feeding the rabbits.

Until this one particular Saturday. Everyone was home, off from work, and children were outside playing as usual. As the afternoon turned into evening, there was noise and commotion coming from the backyard. I remember walking outside to the backyard watching the neighbors, family, and friends rally around my mother. At some point my mom had wondered off by herself into the woods.

They were pleading and begging my mom to come back in the house from the woods. My mom was standing there, alone, in tears and in a fearful state. It was almost like a battle cry. I remember music playing in the background but it wasn't a party. My mom had started playing the music before she walked into the woods.

Music was her voice. Music was her language. It was her expression. I don't remember what song was playing that day, but I know the family was able to talk her out of the woods and my mom survived that episode to live another day. That was my first time remembering something was wrong. Everyone else knew something was wrong too, as they were there to help her. What happened within those moments was beyond my comprehension. What happened to my mom? Why did she wander into the woods? What was her unconscious mind telling her? Why was she the only person who could hear the messages? I went on to play with my friends and cabbage patch dolls like nothing had happened. Until···the next episode!

On the Inside - Mary Jane Girls

"Nothing hurts worse than a heart in pain

And there's nothing more serious

Than when you man's the blame

Hurting on the inside."

Breaking a Continuous Cycle

Memory Lane

Growing up, I watched my mother go through numerous manic-depressive episodes. I didn't know exactly what they were or what was going on. I just knew that there were moments in my life where my mom would turn into a completely different person. She would still be there in her physical body, but the essence of who she really was would disappear. Her voice would change, her appearance, her skin, her behavior, even the look in her eyes. She would morph into a totally different person and go absolutely rogue.

She tried to commit suicide on several occasions. She was often admitted into mental health facilities. When I was around 16 years old, my grandmother called me and told me that she needed to have a difficult conversation with me. She felt I was finally old enough and able to grasp what she was about to tell me.

My grandmother told me that my mother had been molested when she was younger. Not only was she molested, but she was molested by my grandfather, my mother's step-father. The man my grandmother was still married to. The man I called grand-daddy.

My world stopped!

Later on, I found out that my grandmother was also a victim of sexual trauma growing up as a child.

She too, was molested when she was a child by a family member and was impregnated with my mother. After having my mother, my grandmother met my grandfather, they got married, and went on to have five more girls together. My mother was the oldest of the five girls they had together, but my grandfather was not my mother's biological father. My mother was a product of incest and in turn became a victim of incest. A family with toxic patterns.

My grandfather was a hard-working man who took great care of his wife and family. At the time of these events which happened over 20 years prior, my grandmother was still married to my grandfather. So, I didn't anticipate my grandmother divorcing my grandfather. Not after years of marriage, children, grandchildren, great grandchildren and a host of nieces and nephews. I knew that conclusion was off the table. But I couldn't understand why it seemed to be so normalized in my family. Why was I just finding this out at 16? Why weren't any other family members enraged.

We were all a tight knit family. My aunts, uncles, and cousins were always around each other for holidays, birthday parties, special events. This news totally baffled me. How? Who? What? When? Where? Why? All these questions ran through my mind but they wouldn't come out. They couldn't come out. I was raised to be respectful to my elders so I did not question anything my grandmother told me.

It was such an overwhelming experience to hear my grandmother say "No, your mom is not crazy honey, this is what she's experiencing, this is what she went through, and this is the person who did it to her. Oh and yes, we know exactly who did it and you call him 'grand-daddy'."

And that was it! I'm 16 years old, numb, dumb, and confused. My brain couldn't process what I was just told. Happy that I was finally given the missing piece to the puzzle of my life yet but now what I am supposed to do with it?

From that moment, I turned into a psychological investigator. I knew that a phone call wouldn't be the last of what I needed to know about what happened to my mom. My physical, mental, spiritual, and emotional journey with mental health had begun. I wanted answers but knew my family wasn't capable of providing those answers. Obviously, they knew what happened; but no one had responded the way I would've imagined them to respond. This wasn't our regular dinner table conversation. Of all the fun times and excitement, we always had at family gatherings, why was everyone was ok with what happened. Why was no one talking about it? Why was something so obvious, so easy to ignore? It became my elephant in the room.

Summary Notes

CHAPTER ONE

Functional Depression -
Coping Mechanisms

Suppression & How Does it Show Up?

We've all heard of functioning drug addicts. Well, I was definitely a functioning addict of a trauma. Even though the trauma did not directly happen to me, I still developed the behavior of addicts. Denial, excuses, isolation, enabling relationships, loss of memory, and use of substance abuse. My substance abuse of choice was work. I stayed heavily involved with work, church or some type of activity. If I always stayed busy with school, church, or work, there was no time to worry or think about the depression going on in my life. My mother was a functioning addict as well. This was her coping mechanism in her life. Not addressing the hurt, the pain, the suffering, and the confusion made us both functional mental health addicts.

Outside of my mother having these manic-depressive episodes, life was good. We weren't the richest family but we survived alright. We moved a lot because we were not financially stable, but that didn't stop us from living the American dream. On the outside, you would think we were the perfect family. A mother, a father with a daughter and a son, good church going folks who worked hard and loved even harder. Nothing wrong with that picture, right? Because we portrayed that we were such a perfect family, I never knew how to take the time to address the issues on my own.

I was a functional addict. After I received the news from my grandmother of what had actually happened to my mom, I didn't do anything with it. I didn't know what to do with it, so I just lived with it. I wasn't upset nor was I angry. I stopped expressing myself by going numb. I was just your regular, normal-functioning girl going through life. I did not express any emotion to release the anger and confusion. Nevertheless, I remained desperate for answers. I kept it all inside. In my case, being the functional person that I was, I just let it go or at least I thought I did.

In hindsight, it affected every part of my life. Being numb and functional, I didn't realize how much of me I gave away by not expressing myself. I operated from a place of fear. I didn't express it for fear of hurting the people who are involved. Fear of rocking the boat!

Life was normal when my mother wasn't in a manic-depressive state or institutionalized. Everything was going just fine. I became a product of my environment. Hurrying up and getting back to normal as quickly as possible. Knowing this too shall pass, but eventually it would come back to rear with its ugly head again.

Living in Confusion - Phyllis Hyman

"I believed in you
I thought you could do no wrong
Until I saw one day
That you were stringing me along
Played me for a fool
You used me once too much
I'm in so much pain
Here I am again
Trust is a hard thing
To come by these days
You build me up
To let down
Got me spinning around
I wish I knew
Where you were coming from
You told me you loved me
I thought I was your only one
Seems like I'm always going through changes
Living in confusion
Confusion, confusion
Seems like I'm always going through changes
Living in confusion, confusion."

Learned Abuse

Growing up, me nor my brother were strangers to strict discipline. Call it corporal punishment or a good ole ʻwhopping. If you did the crime, you did the time. Even if you didn't do the crime, and were just an observer, you still did the time. But the day when I saw my mother get a whooping was a different story. I remember being in our duplex in the living room, playing. I don't know what my mother did or what the issue was, but I will never forget the look on her face and the look in her eyes, when she was summoned in the room by my father.

She cried and screamed a short yell from her croaked voice. Not so much for herself, but out of the concern that her daughter was witnessing her mother's abuse. She was shoved on the bed as my father proceeded to close the bedroom door and beat her. Whatever the reason or whatever shame she caused for him to beat her; I don't know why. I just sat there innocently, in the living room, powerless and continued to play.

A few years later, we progressed into a better neighborhood. We bought a three-bedroom, two bath home. I remember this being one of the proudest moments for our family. My grandmother, my father's mom even came to live with us for a while. It was the perfect neighborhood. I often went a couple of houses down to play with a neighborhood friend. We would play with barbies and toys in her room. Everything was fine until one day, when I heard yelling and screaming coming from the living room. We both peaked outside the room's door, just in time to see her father dragging her mother across the floor to their bedroom. I looked at her mom, we locked eyes. She had the same look in her eye my mother had when she was abused. My friend went back to playing like she too, was all familiar with the scenario. I sat there stunned, and it was at that moment when I knew that I had learnt the art of ignoring the pain and keeping my mouth shut.

Summary Notes

CHAPTER TWO

Trauma - Here Comes the Boom!

Anger, Hurt, and Fear

Unleash

I never truly allowed myself the time to reflect nor dwell on the flood of emotions within me. For me, it was just anger. I never allowed myself to be angry. The environment I was raised in, did not teach me how to express anger. I was raised in a Christian household, which I interpreted as always forgiving, always happy, always humble. I often denied myself, always putting myself last to help others. I grew a tendency to love others more than myself (which was an oxymoron because I didn't know how to even love myself, let alone love others)

Was it ok to be angry? No. I interrupted anger as a sin. As a Christian, I was taught to forgive. So, I never grieved for myself, my mother, or my grandmother. I never unleashed that emotion. I buried my emotion as an act of forgiveness.

But soon after my functional phase, I became angry. All the questions I had in my mind when I first found out what had happened came rushing back. I wanted answers and I wanted them now. But the sources where I thought I could go to for answers, were not the sources I needed. Everyone involved dealt with this in their own secret quiet way. I imposed the direction of my anger on the people involved, who were not equip to deal with my anger. It was a dangerous and sensitive topic. Not dangerous because it was a taboo subject but dangerous because they weren't able to, or weren't ready to handle my pain. At least not in the way I wanted it handled.

Everyone involved was already in a different space. Some had already processed the event, some moved on and some even made peace with the situation.

But I wanted everyone to feel my pain. I wanted everyone to understand how I felt. I didn't understand that everyone wasn't able or capable to handle my anger, let alone not able to handle what happened. Not everyone was equipped to handle the pain and fear I was ready to release. I did not even consider that they weren't able to process it themselves, so getting angry at them was not going to benefit them or me.

I was looking for solutions and forgiveness in the wrong place, and seeking it from the wrong people. It's not that they weren't willing, but they weren't able to. They didn't understand. It wasn't their pain to understand, and it took me years to understand that it wasn't theirs. It was mine.

Wildflower - New Birth

"She's faced the hardest times you could
imagine
And many times her eyes fought back the tears
And when her youthful world was a
bout to fall in
Each time her slender shoulders bore the weight
of all her fears

And a sorrow no one hears
Still rings in midnight silence, in her ears

Let her cry, for she's a lady
Let her dream, she's a child
Let the rain fall down upon her
She's a free and gentle flower growing wild

And if by chance that I should hold her
Let me hold her for a time
And if allowed just one possession
I would take her in my arms, to be mine

Be careful how you touch her, she'll awaken
As sleep's the only freedom that she knows
And when you walk into her eyes, you won't
believe

The way she's always paying for a debt she never
owes

And a silent wind still blows
That only she can hear, so she goes

Let her cry, oh, she's a lady
Let her dream, 'cause she's a child
Let the rain fall down upon her
She's a free and gentle flower growing wild
She's a flower growing wild, she's a flower
growing wild."

Ending the Pain

Sacrifice

Rough financial times for my family always involved moving. After having to move from the three-bedroom dream house with the pool, we moved a few more times and lived in rental homes. Hurricane Andrew had hit and devastated all the Miami-Dade County. In the aftermath that brought an opportunity to our family. Our church helped my family purchase a home that we were able to call our forever home... for at least a few years.

My mother had become ill again and was in the middle of one of her manic-depressive episodes. I was in high school at the time. My life was okay but my mother's life was not okay. Weeks had gone by, and the mental institution would not admit her. Mental health institutions at the time would interview the potential patient before admitting them. The institution would not admit my mom if she said herself that she as not ill. And they would believe her. She knew how to play upon the system and their emotions. So, our family had to manage with her progressively getting worse and worse. Her symptoms became aggressive, which meant me taking on some adult responsibilities; like cooking and cleaning. We were doing the best we could to take care of her and still live our normal lives.

But one day, something triggered her. She was at the end of her rope. She hadn't slept for days. In this particular home, the hallway led directly from the living room to the bathroom. I never considered the length of this hallway until this day. My mother started running full speed from the living room into the bathroom. There was no way to stop her and besides, I had no idea what she was about to do. She ran into the bathroom, jumped on top of the bathtub, and tried to dive out of the closed bathroom window. She began to aggressively bang her head against the window. She was trying to escape. She wanted to jump out the window. She wanted to escape the noise in her head. She was trying to kill herself.

At that moment, naturally, I jumped to try to stop her and hold her back before she could gash her head. After getting her down from the window and sitting with her, I felt her pain. I connected with her sorrow.

This wasn't my first time seeing my mom try to commit suicide and it wouldn't be the last. I've watched her try to jump out of moving cars. There were times when we had to strategically sit her between two people in the backseat of a car to keep her from jumping out. I've watched my mom run across four lanes of traffic attempting to get hit by a car. But at this moment, I just sat with her and watched her stare out into space knowing that she wanted the pain to go away or end, but there was nowhere for it to go, and it wasn't ending anytime soon. There was nothing I could do but be there for her.

5 am Phone Calls – No Accountability

After my first experience of witnessing (one of many) of one my mother's depressive episodes, I learned what to expect. I began to keenly recognize the signs and symptoms.

One of the symptoms my mother would display were making 5 am phone calls. Before her symptoms would evolve into a full episode, she would start to call my grandfather, the person who had molested her. How ironic that she would reach out to him.

I remember being young and waking up early in morning. She never knew I was listening to her conversation. I'm peeking around the corner to listen to her phone calls, wondering what she would say, and what was on her mind.

The anticipation would kill me. What would she say? Would she get off her chest? Would she finally curse him out?

The conversation was always cordial, short and sweet. A quick five minute "Hi Dad, how are you?" He would respond Hi Lee I'm fine. She would respond that she was fine too. They would maybe discuss current events, say their goodbyes and end the conversation.

My coping mechanism was to laugh. I honestly thought this was funny. It's as if she was calling to tell him that "no" matter how much hurt you caused in my life, I'm still here. I'm still alive. I'm surviving. I'm thriving. He always answered her calls, and he always let her talk. It was her way of reaching out to him before she would enter into one of the darkest moments of her life.

As years, holidays, and family gatherings would come and go, I always admired how my mom could be in a room and share space with the man who molested her. We would gather as a family and act like this act never occurred. Everyone smiled, joked, laughed, played but in the back of my mind, I knew she only participated for the comradery of the family. No one had spoken up or said anything about it before, so why start now? Why was she there? Why did she participate? My conclusions were that she did it for me, for her children, her sisters and her mom. Never considering her emotional or mental well-being as the first priority in her life.

Summary Notes

Intermission

Part Summary Notes

A House Is Not a Home - Luther Vandross

"Doo doo doo doo doo, Doo doo doo doo
doo doo doo doo doo
Doo doo doo doo doo doo doo doo doo, Oh,
oh, oh, oh, oh
A chair is still a chair, even when there's no one
sittin' there
But a chair is not a house and a house is not a
home
When there's no one there to hold you tight
And no one there you can kiss goodnight
Whoa, oh, oh, oh, oh, oh, oh
A room is a still a room, even when there's
nothin' there but gloom
But a room is not a house and a house is not a
home
When the two of us are far apart
And one of us has a broken heart
Now and then I call your name
And suddenly your face appears
But it's just a crazy game
When it ends, it ends in tears
Pretty little darling, have a heart, don't let one
mistake keep us apart
I'm not meant to live alone, turn this house into
a home

When I climb the stairs and turn the key
Oh, please be there, sayin' that you're still in
love with me, yeah
I'm not meant to live alone, turn this house into
a home
When I climb the stairs and turn the key
Oh, please be there, still in love
I said still in love
Still in love with me, yeah
Are you gonna be in love with me
I want you and need to be, yeah
Still in love with me
Say you're gonna be in love with me
It's drivin' me crazy to think that my baby
Couldn't be still in love with me
Are you gonna be, say you're gonna be
Are you gonna be, say you're gonna be
Are you gonna be, say you're gonna be
Well, well, well, well
Still in love, so in love, still in love with me
Are you gonna be
Say that you're gonna be
Still in love with me, yeah
With me, oh, oh, oh, oh, oh."

Summary Notes

CHAPTER THREE

Intimacy and Relationships

My parents met in Goulds, FL, my grandparents literally lived next door to each other. Uniquely, my father's family moved in next door to my mother's. How exquisite to live next door to the soon to be love of your life. Both families grew to know and love each other. My parents got married.

Although we were the perfect family on the outside, watching TV shows and other media outlets gave me the idea that something was wrong. Something was missing. It was intimacy. I grew up in a home that lacked intimacy. Physical touch was not our expression of love. My father was always a hugger but hugs were rare from my mother. My mother was loving and caring but showing affection was not her strong suit. Hugs came from my mother when initiated by someone else. Saying I love you was rarely used in our home. The love was there, we just did not express it physically or verbally

I knew there had to be some form of intimacy in the beginning because my brother and I were conceived. I can only imagine myself as the initiator. I just didn't witness it between my mother and father. Listen, I grew up listening to almost every Luther Vandross song. Barry White was like a great uncle of mine. Al Green and Lou Rawls were imprinted in my brain. Listening to songs, lyrics, and music of this magnitude could only come from a heart filled with warmth, love and intimacy. I knew my parents loved each other but where was the intimacy?

I did not see it growing up. I saw struggle. I saw frustration. I saw miscommunication. I saw loneliness. I saw suppression. I saw a yearning for affection. I saw a yearning for snuggles and kisses. But something was in the way. Something was blocking the physical touch, the warmth, the grace, the lust, the unadulterated touch that only belongs between lovers. The yearning was there, but the physical manifestation of it never happened.

It led me to think where did they learn to love or in better words, where did they learn to be intimate? Did they learn to be intimate? Did they know what intimacy consisted of? Or at least intimacy in the way I saw it portrayed in the movies and on television. Where was that compassion for each other?

My mother's intimacy, love, and compassion was stuck in her childhood where she was sexual violated. Normally, a girl learns to be nurturing, compassionate and cared for by her mother. She learns intimacy, vulnerability, and strength from her father. Fathers and daughters hold a special bond that the father will hopefully pass along to his daughters' mate one day. But my mother's first sexual encounter with the opposite sex was with her father. Unfortunately, my mother never had that experience.

I think my father believed he could love my mother though all her hurts, trauma, and the pain. But my mother's first experience of intimacy was with her step-father. So, how was she supposed to express the same love and intimacy to her husband? How was my father supposed to break down that barrier, blocking what was supposed to be reserved from him? I believe he honestly tried his best. But eventually he gave up and they both ended up suffering in the end. It was a lost cause.

After starting college, my mother discovered my father had an affair. I helped uncover the affair after my father sent me some pictures. Remember, back in the day when pictures were developed, the film negatives also came along with the envelope of pictures. The investigator in me decided to review the negatives. Upon reviewing them, I found pictures that were not included in what was sent to me. They were photos of my father with another woman. They were out together on boats, parties, enjoying each other's company intimately. The intimacy I was waiting to see between my mother and father, I saw between my father and his mistress in those photos.

This was so devastating but not surprising at all. Please do not misconstrue this as me giving my father the right to cheat on his marriage, but I cannot blame him for seeking love, affection, and attention outside of his marriage. It was unavailable to him at home. He was fighting a battle he would not win. The affair cost him a lot in our family, at his job, his business relationships and in the community. He was trying to heal a wounded soul. But he was unequipped and had no idea of the tools required for the job.

Affection, Touch, and Church Hugs

I grew up as a daddy's girl. My father was my superhero. He was tall, handsome, and smart. There was nothing my dad could not do in my eyes. My dad was very affectionate and he found ways to show it. He was lovable by nature. He would initiate hugs or sneak in a cheek kiss. He was my alarm clock for school before cell phones. At the time it irritated me but I loved the way he would walk in my room in the mornings, open the curtain, and sneak and give me a rough grizzly bear kiss on my cheek before he went off to shave for day.

Even throughout adulthood, outside of a boyfriend, my father was always the first person I would call. I knew my dad loved me and I loved him, but there was always a boundary neither one of us crossed. The boundary became crystal clear after that phone call from my grandmother. The stigma of what happened to my mom always loomed over our relationship

Years before we attended a family counseling session. We were meeting with a counselor that was also assigned to my moms' case. My mom was not in attendance for this session. I don't remember how the session started but I will never forget what she asked me. The counselor asked me if I had ever had sex with my father. I was in complete shock as I looked at my father who was sitting across from me. We were both embarrassed. I told the counselor "no". She began to explain that my mother was concerned that my father would sexually assault me since her father has sexually assaulted her. It made since for her to think that way but the damage it did to my fathers and I relationship was not repairable.

From that point on, I only felt comfortable giving my dad "church" hugs. You know the hug where you lean in like you are about to embrace the person but at the last minute you turn your body to the side. There was no such thing as holding hands, no soft caresses, never a chance to just lay my head on his shoulder. Every now and then, he would extend his arms out to me for a hug and a forehead kiss. I made sure to turn my body to not embrace him in a romantic way. Even though my father never put his hands on me or touched me in any sexual way, because it had happened to my mom, I was always careful. Careful for her because naturally, she would think I too, was going to be molested by my father. It was an unspoken protection clause to keep the imagine clear that there was nothing sexual about our relationship.

I missed my lesson on intimacy with my father. More importantly, I missed my father. Yes, we had a great relationship where we could talk, , discuss life, business, or anything. But I missed my dad. The last time I held my dad's hand was on his right before he transitioned. He was already in a coma and couldn't respond, but I knew he could still feel. I wanted to hold his hand one last time, to let him know that although we missed out on all those years of intimacy, I wasn't going to let him go without him knowing that I was no longer afraid to hold his hand.

Relationships

Relationships seemed to come easy for me. I was friends with most of my boyfriends' , so it became natural. I never considered how my upbringing would affect my relationships. As a young girl, I got along well with everyone, boys, family and friends. I dated a couple guys in high school, and the relationships were nice. The often ended mutually.

It wasn't until college that I started to realize two things. I did not know how to be in a relationship. I was always happy and never complained.

I was always the teacher's pet. I became a sponge. The people pleaser. And in turn, I did not know how to reciprocate those feelings. I knew how to be a great listener. I was a great friend that was always there and would do anything for you (actually I was a people pleaser that did almost anything anyone would ask) but I didn't know how to communicate my need and receive.

I was always the giver. Never the taker. I didn't know how to because I didn't understand how to process my feelings and emotions. I didn't know how to advocate for my feelings. I didn't know how to confront for fear of hurting someone's feelings.

The word "no" was not a part of my vocabulary, and I truly thought as long as I did what others said and made them happy, that that was what life was all about. I learned that from my examples.

Naturally, I became promiscuous. I wasn't the town prostitute but I had my fair share of relationships in college. Promiscuity became my intimacy.

The more I longed for it, the more promiscuous I became. I was filling the void for the intimacy I lacked with my father in men. I learned what I saw. Without any feelings attached to it, I taught myself intimacy, or so I thought I did.

I didn't know how to show compassion. Most importantly, I didn't know how to be intimate. Was I compassionate? Yes, but those are two different things.

Marriage

After graduating college and dating some more, I met my husband. We immediately fell in love and knew that we were going to be together. In the beginning, everything was beautiful as we were getting to know each other. But my fiancé at the time quickly saw the emotional wall I too had built up just like my mother did with my father. Of course, I was head over heels in love with this man but something was holding me back. This was uncharted territory.

The saying that every girl marries her father was definitely true in my case. My husband is so caring and thoughtful. Affection and touch are one of his love languages. The patterns from my childhood began to play out into my marriage. I did see my dad attempt to display affection and touch, but my mom's response was distant and stoic. I began to fall into the same pattern that was displayed to me, until my husband called me on it. Thank God!

That was my wake-up call. It was a tough pill to swallow but I could not continue the pattern. I already had a living example of how that scenario turned out through my parent's marriage. I had to learn to not only give affection and love through touch, but also how to receive it. How to receive love. What a gift!

Summary Notes

CHAPTER FOUR

No One's Coming to Save You – Mental Illness – It's Insanity to Think Otherwise

Visiting Day

Visiting hours in the mental health institution were very limited amounts of time. They were usually a three-hour period in the morning or a three hours period in the evening. My father made sure we visited my mom on a regular basis. This particular visit was different.

I remember getting ready to go visit my mom after she had been admitted. Weeks and sometimes months would go by, yet the moment I knew that I was going to visit my mom made it special. I already had the expectation set in my mind what would happen once I would see her. The medications should be working in her brain and she would be my normal mom again. We will run to each other, embrace each other and the doctors would give a diagnosis that eventually she would be coming home. But that was not the case.

When we first walk in mental health institution, it's almost set up like a jail. Before you can go in, you have to make sure you don't have any metal objects or anything on you that the patient may take to hurt themselves or others. There are several doors and hallways you'd have to go through before you can get to the patients. And finally, from there onwards, you get to the patient area, a huge room at this particular facility that has several beds lined down a wall in rows, separated by curtains. I could see the beds from where I stood on the other side of the desk counter. Each bed had one small drawer that the patient could put their belongings in. The floor was cold. The room was cold.

The technicians stayed behind the desk doing their paperwork. While the patients were able to walk freely, or either congregate in the area near the TV. I remember spotting my mom, and she recognized us. But that intimate embrace that I was longing for did not occur.

My mom knew who I was. But I wasn't her daughter at the moment. I was someone coming to visit her in a mental health institution. She came over to greet me and my father. We brought her some things and some of her belongings for her to keep while she was staying there. She came over to us, with no type of expression, no emotion whatso ever. She spoke but seemed more interested in getting back to new found "friends" in the mental health institution.

At this point, I realized my mom knew that she was on her own. My mother knew no one was coming to save her. She knew no one understand her pain. Not that she wasn't happy to have family to come see her and support her, but that her healing journey was hers and hers alone. This wasn't her first time being admitted and it wasn't going to be her last either. This was a lifelong process. So, she had to figure out her own coping mechanisms. When there was nothing else her family or friends could do for her, she had to be admitted. What could she lean on, and to whom could she turn to?

The other patients in the facility understood her, and she understood them. There seemed to be an unspoken language understood by them all. A language that was layered in hurt, abuse and ambiguity.

The visit didn't last for more than ten minutes. Nevertheless, I was disappointed because I didn't visit my mom that day. I visited a mental health patient who was more excited to go spend time with her "friends" than to spend time with her husband and her daughter. It hurt to watch her walk away. But I knew she was not ready to come home.

Later on, in life I realized the lack of emotion and unhappiness was not directed towards me. It was her survival method. It was the only way she would survive the time she had to spend with strangers, away from her family.

Who Knows You Better Than YOU?

Everyone has seven basic needs to live a healthy, functional life. When one of these is not met, something or someone will evolve to replace it to survive. Those basic needs are physiological, safety, love, truth, esteem, power, alignment, and connection. See Attachment 1 – Maslow's Hierarchy of Needs

In my mother's case, the seeds of these needs were planted but only a few of them were watered. Her early childhood physiological needs were met. Missing out on the basic needs in life is enough to drive anyone into insanity. To survive, my mother had to figure out how to replace the love, truth, esteem, power, alignment, and connection in her life. Those same missing needs were passed down to me.

Children expect their parents to fulfill all their needs. To be their emotional and physical support growing up in life. Because of the emotional trauma inherited in my bloodline, that was not the case in my mother's upbringing. Subsequently she only had so much to pass on to me and my siblings. But it wasn't her fault. She provided us with all the motherly skills she herself that her mother and grandmother, were raised with. They didn't know any better. They were doing the best they could with what they had and with what they were taught.

I cannot imagine the turmoil and grief my mom experienced being abused by her step-father and ignored by her mother. I cannot imagine the feelings of abandonment, loneliness, guilt, grief, and shame she carried on her entire life.

But I do know she used that abandonment, loneliness, guilt, grief, and shame to build her wall of survival. To survive that amount of pain and not express it, you have to be emotionally tough, building a shield of protection to keep anyone else from hurting you again. Especially, if it the people who were supposed to protect you are your parents, and are at the root of your pain.

I know those 5 am phone calls were her way of releasing her pain and fear. She had to release. All while my mother's needs were sacrificed. She was the sacrificial lamb.

What do you do with that? How do you process that? Where is the love? Are you even loved or are you being tolerated? How do you learn to love yourself, let alone others when you were set aside as the sacrificial lamb? My mother's sanity was sacrificed to keep the family together. She paid the price her entire life by going mentally ill to keep the perfect family image.

What could she do? Who could she turn to? The one person she thought she could trust; her mother had already made her decision crystal clear. Her own mother deserted her in an unhealthy physiological environment to be raised in. Her sanity was not worth the price. So, she held it in. She held it in as much as she could until something would trigger her to release and let the world feel her hurt, guilt and pain. That's all she had. No one was coming to save her. So, she had to break down to release it.

Her alter ego, the woman she turned into when something would trigger her into mental illness was her shield. This person was the total opposite of the mother I knew.

Let's call her "Lil Lee" for reference. When Lil Lee came out, it was no holds barred. Leona, my mother was a sweet, calm, quiet, reserved. Lil Lee was the complete opposite. Lil Lee was full of anger. Lil Lee cursed, yelled, screamed, and whatever else she felt like doing. Lil Lee would let you have it and not think about the consequences. You wouldn't dare and try to win a stare down contest with Lil Lee. There was no way you would win.

I learned how to separate my two moms, and I quickly learned how to interact with them. Lil Lee wanted someone to listen to her. Lil Lee wanted to be taken seriously. Lil Lee did not want to be second guessed or questioned because that meant something was wrong with her. I learned how to think two steps ahead to avoid saying something that would trigger Lil Lee or make her upset. I learned how to play the mind game.

When she wasn't attempting to kill herself, I enjoyed Lil Lee. I enjoyed her jovial spirit. I know what I most enjoyed was her honesty. Everything that Leona, my regular mother held in, Lil Lee exposed. Witnessing that type of freedom and honesty from my mother was refreshing because I knew that's what she needed to release as part of her healing.

One of the most dangerous things you can do in the healing process is seeking the answers outside of yourself. Expecting someone to come save you. There are no saviors. No one is coming to save you.

Waiting for a savior outside of you. Expecting someone outside of you to help you deal with the pain can be very difficult. The pain and hurt that has been endured, must be confronted and dealt with. Being vulnerable, hurt and pain is a delicate, sensitive place. Entrusting that hurt and pain into someone who's not qualified and does not have the tools or capacity to handle that hurt and pain can lead to a path, of destruction.

Especially in my case were anger was involved. I expected someone outside of me to come fix that anger that was inside of me. Outside of a certified therapist, sangoma, or initiated chief, It's not their job.

My mother didn't realize how powerful she was. I truly believe if my mother had been given the right treatment and healed her trauma, she would've lived a life where she put herself first before anyone else's pain unapologetically

Before I began my healing journey, I didn't realize how powerful I was. I gave a lot of my power away and expected other people to be able to do the hard work, and handle my pain.

In theory for me and my mom, we both already felt defeated. We already felt like the world was against us because of our situation. Instead of thinking that I was strong enough to be able to get over this, the thought of giving that burden to somebody else sounded so easy but simultaneously giving your power away. Ultimately, I learned through my training and studying my ancestral lineage that I empower the same healing energies my ancestors held. I have the power within myself. My mother had the power within herself too, she just didn't have a chance to tap into it.

Bridge
I Want to Be Free - Ohio Players

"One day child, I won't have to listen to your lies
On that day, I'll be able to make up my own mind
You know, I think I done finally realized
And now I think I can put you out of my life
I'm gonna be free! (I want to be free to run away)
I'm gonna be free! (I want to be free to run away)
I'm gonna be free! (I want to be free to speak my mind, all the time)
I want to be free!
I want to be free!
I want to be free!
And one morning,
I won't be afraid to leave.
And all those things that you told me,
I never could conceive.
I'm gonna be free! (I want to be free to run away)
I'm gonna be free! (I want to be free to run away)
I'm gonna be free! (I want to be free to speak my mind, all the time)
I want to be free!
I want to be free!
I want to be free!

I want to be free!

I want to be free!

You don't know how it makes me feel child,

To be able to walk away from your smile.

And I'm gonna be alright, after a while.

I think the Lord done gave me a strength now.

*I'm gonna be free! (I want to be free to run
away)*

*I'm gonna be free! (I want to be free to run
away)*

*I'm gonna be free! (I want to be free to speak
my mind, all the time)* "

Summary Notes

CHAPTER FIVE

Healing the Soul – Spirit of Release

My path to ancestral healing and self-discovery began while following Art Cathey, a compelling influencer on YouTube, I began to understand how ancestral reverence was such an important missing piece of my life. I listened as she described how our communication with our ancestral roots was the missing link to discovering our missions in life and uncovering our purpose. Hesitant to move forward in learning more, I continued to sit on the sidelines and watch more videos until finally I decided to enroll in a course. I took my first course with Chief Montana and the Ancestral Way Community (ARC). It was within the ancestral way community that I learned the tools needed to communicate with the ancestral realm.

As I studied, listened, and participated, the missing pieces of my life began to reveal themselves and my past made more sense. I had several divinations. The family I was born into, my desires, my mission, my purpose, all the events that had taken place earlier in my life, it all began to make sense. I was born into a family of healers. My nurturing spirit resonated with what the divinations were telling me.

Imagine being able to communicate with your great grandmother who has transitioned years ago just as if she is sitting right there with you, or receiving a message from your great grandfather confirming that you are on the right path, and that he will assist you with your needs. This is the experience that comes with ancestral communication. I began having dreams of ancestors known and unknown. I received messages from my father who had transitioned in 2016. I began to learn how to communicate with my family.

I had my very own ancestral warrior team. An ancestral warrior team that had been waiting for me to surrender to the idea of living this life in fear, shame, regret, confusion, and doubt. I was ready to lay all that down to finally receive guidance and the answers to questions I had with me for years, and to put my ancestors to work on mine and my family's behalf.

What Does it Take to Heal? Does Everyone Deserve a Chance to Heal?

Innovate

What does it take to process, confront and heal from trauma? Western society often teaches us to avoid taking responsibility for, our actions, our temperament, , and our own healing. We have been trained to look outside of ourselves for help. To doubt ourselves; our mind, our intuition, our thoughts, our ways of knowing, our intellect, our beauty, our morals, our standards, our commitments, and our very essence of being. Co-dependent on the need to seek outside ourselves and ask experts how to discover ourselves.

The answer is within you. You already have the answers to all the questions. It's a matter of remembering who you are and whose you are. Often, we were taught that we were born as sinners, born inadequate, unfulfilled, and as filthy rags. Confusion, turmoil, and anxiety is what keeps our lives in pain, suffering, agony, anxiety and defeat. Then we spend the majority of our lives trying to fill the void, confused, disturbed, and anxiously trying to fulfill a divine contract that we never knew existed.

A divine contract between the creator, God and yourself was established for you to even exist in the earthly realm.

READ THIS OUT LOUD:

"I have the power within myself alone. My ancestors are all knowing. I come from a blood line of strong individuals. I come from a bloodline of warriors and healers, and they are all inside of me. I am enough on my own."

Until I began to understand my ancestral lineage, I did not know where I came from and without not knowing my ancestral lineage, I was unaware of the power that I held. My future and the expectations were all tied to something outside of myself.

How can you avoid making this mistake? Have patience, grace and mercy on yourself. It takes time. Learn how to have the utmost patience, with yourself first. First patience with yourself, patience with your past, patience with your future and then patience with others. You have to sit down with···wait for it − You! Sit down, check in, analyze, and calibrate yourself.

Sit down with yourself and allow those triggers to come up. Dig up those bigger emotions. Where were you when it happened? How old were you when it happened?

What was around you? Were there any objects, sounds, or smells in the room or around you. Who was with you? How did you feel? What happened next? Where did you go or what did you do?

Go back to that moment in time, where you were not in control. Go to that place to honor and respect that moment. Not to place it on a pedestal but to free it from the bondage in your mind that continues to haunt, replay, and torture you till this day.

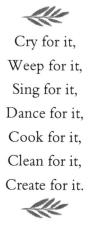

Cry for it,
Weep for it,
Sing for it,
Dance for it,
Cook for it,
Clean for it,
Create for it.

Seek those creative outlets to get the anger out, put the anger into your outlets, and to your dance, into your music, and into your poetry because just by putting it into the people who may not be able to understand and handle your pain can be colossal.

Release

As a child, because of my mother's insecurities, I didn't think I was enough. I didn't think I was beautiful although people told me all the time how pretty I was. I carried a very low self-esteem and always felt the need for an outside entity to help boost my confidence.

My mother was a very beautiful woman as well, but rarely invested in herself. We took care of ourselves hygienically but often times it was the bare minimum. We did some girly things like going to the hairdresser on a regular basis but that was the basis of our self-care routine. My mother never went to get her nails done. She wore basic foundation, one color of lipstick which was a basic red, and kept a very minimal makeup routine. She had two favorite perfumes: Elizabeth Arden Red Door or White Diamonds by Elizabeth Taylor.

She rarely went on girls dates or out to eat with her girlfriends on the weekend. I do remember going with my mother to her friend's houses on the weekends to talk and gossip. These friends were also members of our church, so there was never any alcohol or drugs involved. That was her get away. She took care of her husband, her children, and her home. Who took care of her?

I got my first job when I was 16. Still being of the frugal mindset, I began to buy items for myself. I purchased my school clothes. I started to get my nails done on a regular basis. I continued to work throughout college and began to treat my mom on birthdays and holidays. I knew it but it became more apparent how much she put others before herself. I began to question where did this spirit come from? The idea that it was ok to neglect yourself to make sure everyone else is okay? I made a decision that this was not going to be my reality. The spirits that haunted my mother would not haunt me. I had to make a mental shift in my mind that I was worthy. I had to release those inferior spirits.

I had to release the spirit of lack, the spirit of poverty, the spirit of unworthiness, the spirit of self-doubt, and the spirit of always doing for others while neglecting yourself. Release the spirit of not honoring my feelings, my anger, my pain. Allowing all those feelings to flow freely. Release the spirit to please others because I'm too uncomfortable making them upset. Release the spirit of being perfect. Release the spirit of denying me.

I Will Take Care of You

In 2014, my father was diagnosed with stage four colon cancer. You would never know he was battling this disease by the way he carried himself, and still managed his life. He took care of my mother and my little brother, who was in high school at the time. In 2015, the cancer progressed after radiation and chemotherapy treatments, and his body began to deteriorate but he still worked, ran errands, visited the family, and attended church. In early 2019, he was hospitalized for the last time and the doctors placed him in hospice.

We all agreed to bring him home to live the last days of his life. If you have ever experienced being with a person in hospice; although, you know they are going to transition, just the thought of them physically still being there and breathing brought some relief to us as a family. I was able to tell my father how much I loved him, how proud I was to be his daughter, and that he did not have to suffer anymore. I gave him the permission to pass away.

An hour later my father took his last breath, I tried to brace myself before walking into the room to see his body without life and without breath, but there is nothing that can prepare you for that moment. As I braced myself, I was also very aware of my mother losing the love of her life. I knew this was going to be an uphill battle for her and her mental health. As we walked into the room, my body released all the emotions I had been holding in for the last couple of weeks. I wept. At the same time, my mother's soul opened up. I heard a scream of release that she had been holding onto for years. I never heard my mother cry like that. She had lost the love of her life.

As the family began to gather and mourn, immediately, everyone's concern was on my mother's mental health. We automatically assumed that if anything would send her into another episode, this was definitely going to send her back to a mental home. But to all of our surprise, weeks went by, we funeralized my father, months went by and my mother did not get sick. She did not go mentally insane after my father transitioned. My father's death was not a trigger for her. She maintained her mental sanity, and continued to be a mother to me and my brothers.

After my father transitioned, she slowly started to deteriorate herself. Her soul mate was gone. After fracturing her hip, living in a rehabilitation home for several months, and starting dialysis treatments, I knew I had to bring my mom home with me. I couldn't bear the thought of all her remaining life in a group home after all her contributions to me and our family.

So, my husband and I bought a home fit to bring my mom home. She was so happy. She was more excited for us buying the home than I was. It was the least I could do after all she had sacrificed over the years. On top of buying a home, I knew she would need in-home personal care so I started a home healthcare business to be able to hire a family whom I knew, who would give her the first- class care she deserved. I knew I would need to help to take care of her but what I didn't consider was my emotional, physical and mental well-being. The doctor's visits, scheduling in home care, weekly dialysis visits, the cardiologist visits, the surgeries, and the emergency room visits. I was exhausted but I was determined to keep going. My mom never gave up on me so I was not going to give up on her.

One night a couple of months before she transitioned, I was in the kitchen and she came out of her room with her walker. I was tired as usual, but was still preparing dinner and making sure she had everything she needed for her dialysis appointment the next day. I was her caregiver but she was still my mother, so when I wanted to vent, we would talk. I began to tell her how exhausted I was. I said "Mom, I'm tired. Work, taking care of the house, and taking care of you comes with a load of responsibility. I'm tired but I can't stop. I can't stop because who's gonna take care of my husband, the house, etc. and I don't have anyone to take care of me.

Who's gonna take care of me?"

I'll never forget the look of her face as she was standing there with her walker, her soft voice as she looked at me and said, "I'll take care of you."

At that moment, I wanted to laugh it off but I just smirked thinking, lady, how are you gonna take care of me when I take care of you? But her words couldn't be any truer today than they were then. She is living up to her words. She is taking care of me. Her presence is so much more powerful in the ancestral realm. She is a black girl magic. Her transition became so much bigger than me.

After she transitioned, I understood that she had to leave. She was my clutch. She was my excuse. As long as I was busy taking care of her, I would never pursue my dreams. She knew she had to go to give me permission to be who I was born to be. With her here, I would still be reluctant, scared, limited, and bound. Bounded by her sickness, her disability, and her worry. When her soul left this earth, I became free. Free to be me. Free to write this story in honor of her and my grandmother's legacy.

It's Not Normal to Suffer

In African tradition, it its taught that we are not born into a world of suffering, pain. Western society has conditioned us to believe that life is supposed to be hard. If we aren't suffering or going through something, then we must not be doing life right. But that idea of thought in ancestral ideology is not true. We are born into the world whole and complete. We were not born to suffer. We were born to fulfill our purpose and live our lives to the best of our abilities.

Yet life happens. Now in our western perspective, we tend to accept things the way they are, ignore our past, and live thinking we are deemed to endure suffering and pain. From an ancestral perspective, when life happens; we stop. Stop to take the time to listen. Listen for the message that the life event is calling you to. Have a divination. Listen for your ancestors calling on the root cause of the situation and how it should be resolved.

GIVE YOURSELF PERMISSION TO HEAL. Allow yourself to be vulnerable to the Process. This is a lifelong process that I'm going through. I had to take each emotion that I was going through and break that down, and sometimes those emotions took years to get through, so this is absolutely a life-long work; a lifelong process.

To heal, you first need to accept and acknowledge that something is broken. If it ain't broke, don't try to fix it...right? To pick up the pieces of your life, you must admit your life is in pieces. Each piece represents something that has been impacted by the damage. Dissecting each piece into its own category by giving it the proper attention it deserves will serve your healing. What do those pieces look like? Give each piece its rightful energy which it deserves to be released and reformed into whatever it is intended to be. Energy forms into something, it becomes behavior which is its intended job, and then it returns back to energy. It has to go somewhere. Now you have the choice to decide where it goes, how it goes, who it goes to, and why it should go? Before you were not aware, you had a choice. Now, you do! It is not a matter of if it shows up, but how does it show up for you? Is it anger? If it is anger, you are not angry alone. Your anger and assortment of feelings have a meaning and a reason.

《 》Is it anxiety?

《 》Is it low self-esteem?

《 》Is it confusion?

《 》Is it pain?

《 》Is it health related or a medical complication?

《 》Is it your spouse or your children?

《 》Is it relationship issues?

《 》Is it self-sabotage?

《 》Is it erratic behavior?

《 》Is it fear?

《 》Is it resentment?

《 》Is it self-delete page?

Suffering is a part of greatness but let's not normalize it.

Some safe, effective outlets include: Meditation, prayer, singing, dancing, poetry, that creative expression, and then on top of that, your spiritual tools, connecting with your ancestors, and connecting with your blood line to understand your life story. Verse six discusses tools you can use to connect with your ancestors.

If there is no one to talk to, if there is nowhere to go, there needs to be an outlet, there has to be a way for it to be expressed, whether it's through poetry, through writing, through music, some way that emotions needs to get out, and be expressed. My mother's outlet was music and the mental illness.

Be patient with yourself. We didn't ask for these situations to happen. We didn't deserve some of the things that have happened to us, but they still happened. Have grace and mercy on yourself, have grace and mercy for others; it's a process and it takes time, just be patient.

Summary Notes

CHAPTER SIX

Ancestral Communication

Create

Our life is a story whether we want to accept it or not, there's a story there, for whatever reason or events that have happened were placed into my story and your story.

The connection, the tools of connecting with your ancestors through, meditation, connecting with nature, grounding, or even if you have an altar or shrine. Keeping that connection going helps to get a better understanding of life, your purpose, and mission. Our ancestors are here to help us fulfill our purpose, navigate through life, and to govern and mend our relationships.

Spiritually, mentally, physically, and emotionally, ancestors know what you've been through and they know exactly what to do to correct it. They do not exist to hurt or put you in harm's way. Just as a reminder that you come from greatness, to never fear as you are superior and you're here on this earth for a divine purpose. Knowing that deep in your heart, keeping that with you to combat whatever you face, whatever has come your way, and just to keep that as a shield to protect you from it all.

You have to make a decision. You have to make a decision on what you are going to do with this new-found information. Where are you going to take action or are going to sit back and let it go.

When you're healing, you need to understand the root cause and get a better understanding of why. The ancestral piece of it, understanding your bloodline, understanding who you come from, where you come from, and what you were born in this world to be, to feel the trauma.

What is ancestral communication?

Ancestral communication with the ancestral realm provides guidance, support, love, and direction for all our earthly needs.

Why do we need ancestral communication?

We need ancestral communication because our souls need exploration. Our souls need exploration through life. Our ancestors exist to help us explore through life by helping us fulfill our purpose, navigate through life, and help govern & mend our relationships.

How did our families get in the positions they are in?

How did we become so disconnected?

We lost connection with our source.

What is the source?

The source is our history. Our family. Our bloodline. The source is our own power. We now call it intuition or discernment. Our spiritual roots and traditions were stripped away from us to disconnect us from our innate power to help guide and maneuver gracefully in life.

We disconnected from the entity that brought us here and within us holds the story of our entire being. Parents, grandparents, great grandparents, great grandparents, and it continues down the line. We have entire lineages of wealth and knowledge to tap into.

But it goes untapped, unnoticed, and unutilized. Rituals connect us back to the source, the connection our families are so desperately in need of. All our answers are tied back to source. They have the answers to all our unanswered questions. Our ancestors have experienced everything, and anything we are going through struggling with. There is nothing new under the sun. They are our guides. We need to begin to use them. They are waiting for us to use them.

How do we use them? Here are a few ways you can connect with your ancestral lineage.

Developing a close relationship with your ancestors helps you to know what offerings they like and want. You can strengthen this relationship by doing regular invocations. You start each ritual by invoking your ancestors. Call upon them by their individual names. Tell them to come forth. Ask them to bring forth all the known but forgotten ancestors.

Ask them to bring forth clean ancestors. Examples of unclean ancestors include those who have committed suicide. Your ancestors will know who to call upon and will filter the clean ancestors from the unclean for you.

Call special attention to your great grandparents. Tell them to come forth to reestablish a tradition that has long been lost. Ask them to reestablish partnership with you. Ask them to clear the pathway for your bloodline. Ask them to stand behind you because you are here to fulfill upon your purpose and you cannot do that without their assistance.

Tell them you need their assistance in cleaning up your bloodline, so that your family can once again be whole and complete. You want your family to be suitable to bring forth great ancestors. Trust the process. Release control of what you think it's going to look like and allow life to happen. You are the ritual.

Water/Bowl Method

You'll need:

《 》 Fresh water (Spring, alkaline – No faucet water)
《 》 A calabash or a bowl. A new bowl never used before made of original material: glass, wood, natural material (no plastic or synthetic materials).

Pour the fresh water in the bowl, start flicking the water from the bowl. Flick the water on the ground, floor, or on a plant. Start calling upon your ancestors. Speak to them and tell them what you are calling them forth for. Continue flicking the water as long as you are speaking. Be present and intentional.

End your invocation with Ase'

Dreams

Pay attention to your dreams. Dreams are a form of communication in the ancestral realm. Pay attention to them. They are messages.

Meditation/Prayer

Mediate and pray to yourself. Sit with yourself. Sitting quietly with just you and your thoughts.

Reciprocity

Candles, incense and water are a few offerings that can be used to show reciprocity and fuel your ancestors to work on your behalf

Candles/Incense

《 》 White candle- can be used to state an intention like (giving thanks, calling forth peace, happiness, clarity etc.), for self or someone else. It's for giving instructions to your ancestors to do something.

《 》 Red candle- is often used to strengthen your ancestors to fulfill your request.

《 》 Incense- are often used to add sweetness or ease to an intention that you are stating.

Alter/Shrine

Dedicating a space specifically for ancestral reverence. A sacred space for communication.

Other Forms/Outlets

If the spirit is not grounded, centered and rooted − it becomes vulnerable to other beings. A chief or a sangoma can help you navigate the ancestral realm.

A sangoma is a practitioner of ngoma, a philosophy based on a belief in ancestral spirits and the practice of traditional African medicine, which is often a mix of medicinal plants and various animal body fats or skin

Sangomas listen to spirit to eradicate the root cause of the disease altogether. Depression = Emptiness= Not being connected to your roots. Suicide is direct correlation to not being rooted and grounded. If you deny what you are here to do or say you deny "life" ! You need to be rooted and grounded.

MUSIC/DANCE

Healing through music & dance

Prayer − Affirmations − Intentions

Do you know the greatness from which you've come? "Know thyself" .

Naim Akbar

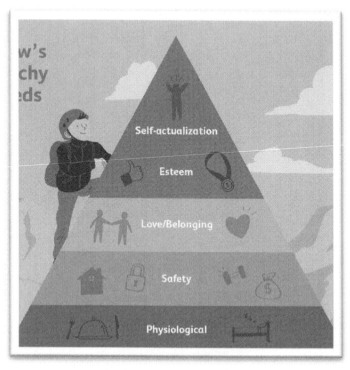

Maslow's Hierarchy of Needs
Seven Basic Essential Human Needs

《》PHYSIOLOGICAL NEEDS – Our biological needs for healthy food, water, air, clothing, exercise, freedom from pain, and sex.

《》SAFETY AND STABILITY NEEDS – Our biological need for safety, for a safe home, safe spaces, secure finances, consistency, and stability. Safety includes the absence of assault of any kind, including physical assault (e.g.

spanking), emotional assault, and psychological assault. Stability includes the emotional consistency of stable parental relationships. Financial stability includes resources sufficient to remove the anxieties and uncertainties of survival.

《》LOVE/BELONGING NEEDS – Our biological need for unconditional support, acceptance, and inclusion. Our biological need to feel we are wanted and connected to something. We all need to feel that we belong.

《》TRUTH/UNDERSTANDING NEEDS – Our biological need for truth and understanding. We see this biological need emerge early, as children ask all sorts of questions. "Mommy, why is the sky blue?" "Daddy, why are you angry all the time?" As Maslow said, we all have a biological drive to know and understand the world.

《》ESTEEM/POWER – Our biological need to feel good about ourselves. Our biological need to feel powerful and efficacious, like we can control the world we live in and create the world we want.

《》ALIGNMENT WITH HIGHEST SELF – Our biological need to be in alignment with and fully express our highest and best self. In Humanistic Psychology, this is known as self-actualization (A. H. Maslow 1971; Daniels 1982). The need to align, the need to self-actualize, is a "universal aspect of human nature," a basic "impulse to grow, to enhance and actualize itself, and to be all that one is capable of becoming" (Abraham H. Maslow, 1991).

《》CONNECTION – our biological need to express and connect with our highest self. In Transpersonal Psychology, this is known as transcendence; in Christianity and Islamic traditions, this is known as salvation, "Entering the Kingdom" etc. (In Buddhism and Eastern traditions, enlightenment). In Sociology, this notion is expressed in a Christian form in Troelstech's conception of mysticism as the "perfection of the spiritual life" and "unity with the divine." (Steeman, 1975) Evelyn Underhill points directly to this need when she says that "we have an innate tendency…towards complete harmony with the transcendental order, whatever the theological formula under which that order is understood" (Underhill. 2002).

BOOK NOTES

Soul Confessions: Ancestral Healing Workbook

Who are you?

Where did you come from?

What are you made of?

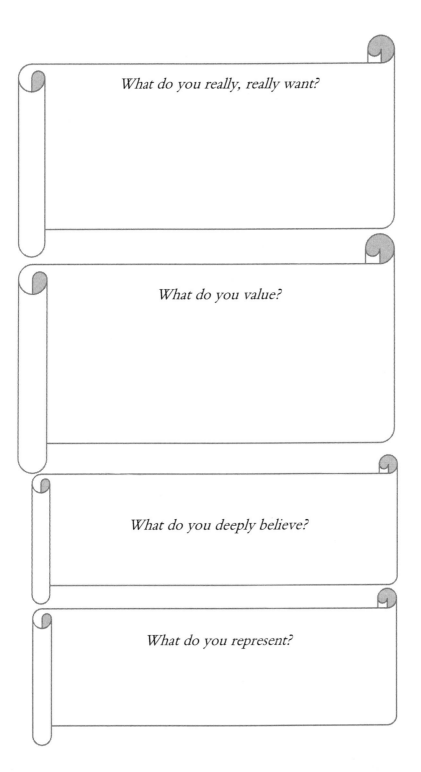

What do you really, really want?

What do you value?

What do you deeply believe?

What do you represent?

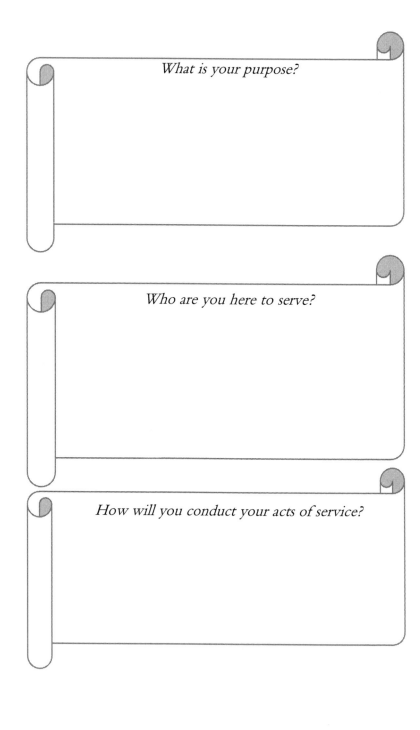

What is your purpose?

Who are you here to serve?

How will you conduct your acts of service?

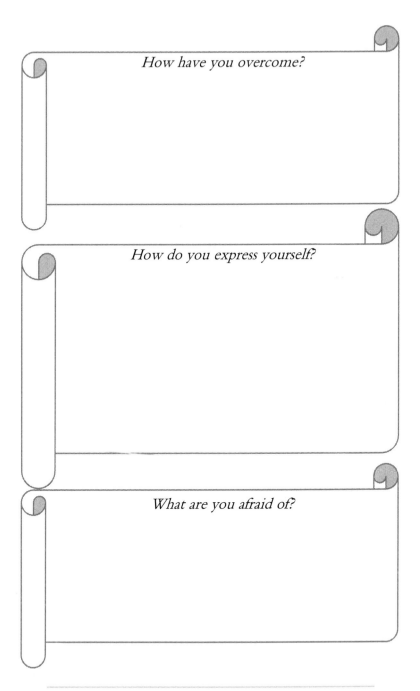

How have you overcome?

How do you express yourself?

What are you afraid of?

What do you know now that you didn't before about how spiritual residue and the implications on your life? From the moment your soul was opened up, bound by spirits.

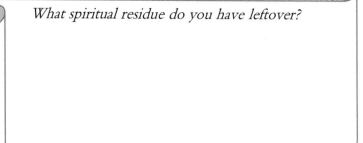

What spiritual residue do you have leftover?

How have you judged yourself?
What do you forgive yourself for?
What do you appreciate yourself for?
Summarize it all: What are your 5 P's?
Purpose, Plans, Passion, Pain, Power

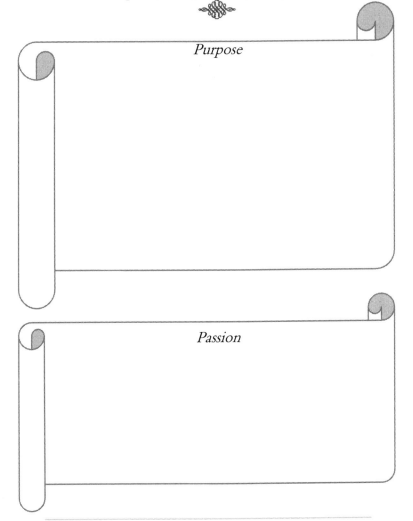

Purpose

Passion

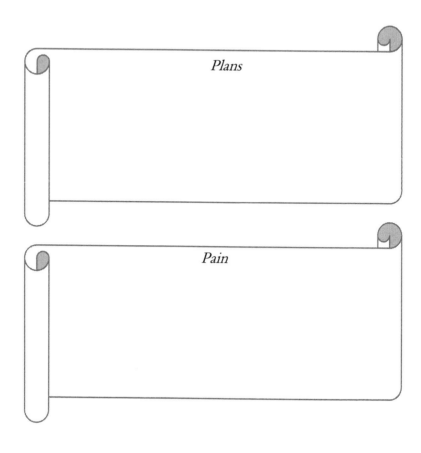

Plans

Pain

Power

Once you hear the voice within answer, it's
time for you to create a plan for your life and
begin making choices and taking actions that will
get you there. Live your life authentically being
you by aligning these answers with your
behaviors.

Meet Cassandra James Gant

Cassandra James Gant is an expert in Process, Confront, and Heal. Her accomplishments include:

Education

Studied Psychology in High School & College.
Bachelor of Science in Business Administration.
Studied Ancestral Communication at the Ancestral Renewal and Communication school. https://chiefmontana.com/

Work History

Second Grade Elementary School Teacher.
Nuclear Analyst at Power Plant.

Personal Life

Daughter of Bipolar Schizophrenic.

Living with a bipolar schizophrenic mother, witnessing her living in mental health facilities, and dealing with the emotional damage done to everyone involved.

Cassandra decided to let go of her fear of not being supported in telling my mother's story, Fear of not having someone's approval before making a decision, and no fear of saying no. Most of what you need is instruction and encouragement from someone who has "been there and done that!" with how to transform the pain in your life to passion using ancient ancestral tools to reclaim your dignity and find your purpose.

And as you can see, Process, Confront, and Heal expert Cassandra James Gant is uniquely qualified to help you understand everything you need to know about how to process your thoughts, get to the root cause, confront your pain, and heal!

Notes

About the Author

Cassandra James Gant is a well-known expert on the subject of processing, confronting and healing and has graciously consented to share her extensive knowledge and experience to help share how she avoided the most damaging mistakes in this area. This is for every survivor, caregiver to survivors of molestation, rape and trauma so you can understand the trauma, how to transform the pain in your life to passion using ancient ancestral tools to reclaim your dignity and find your purpose.

My name is Cassandra James Gant, daughter of Leona Harrison James, a bipolar schizophrenic survivor of molestation and rape. Leona is the daughter of Ida Ethel Harrison Burgess, a survivor of molestation and rape. I was born and raised in Sunny Miami, Florida. My parents originally are from the deep south state of South Carolina. My mother was conceived out of incest by grandmother, and another family member in South Carolina. That family member never claimed my mother as his own so I never had a chance to get to know that side of my family, at least not from a grand daughter's perspective. Both sets of my grandparents migrated here when they were younger, so my parents lived in Miami for majority of their lives.

My father worked in real estate, insurance, car sales, community development, you name it – he did it – Jack of all trades or should I say Joe of all trades. His name was Joseph. He was my superhero who always knew who, what, when, where, and how to make things happen. My mother was always a nurturer.

She loved children and I've always been raised with my mom caring for nurturing children. She worked as a teacher's assistant, several daycare centers, and even kept a small number of children at home for several years. I would love coming home from school because I knew someone's child was going to be there and I always felt like I had a little brother or sister to come home to. In my freshman year of college, I finally got that little brother. My mom decided to adopt her forever baby.

While in high school, I developed an interest in psychology due to my mother's mental illness. I decided to take some psychology classes. I had to and wanted to learn more about the mind and the way it worked. I wanted to heal my mom. When I went on to college, I took some more psychology classes, but never presumed it as a career due to financial reasons. I ended up majoring in Business Administration. Over the years while looking for steady employment, I inherited the same nurturing spirit from my mother's and worked at day care centers and taught second grade for a year. I'm currently a business analyst with a local power company.

This story was inspired by releasing her fears. Fear of not being supported in telling my mother's story, Fear of not having someone's approval before making a decision, and no fear of saying no. Cassandra understands that Most of what we all need is instruction and encouragement from someone who has "been there and done that!" with how to transform the pain in your life to passion using ancient ancestral tools to reclaim your dignity and find your purpose.

And as you can see, Process, Confront, and Heal expert Cassandra James Gant is uniquely qualified to help you understand everything you need to know about how to process your thoughts, get to the root cause, confront your pain, and heal!

Now that we've got that out of the way, let us dive into those mistakes in the cycle of processing, confronting and healing that I've made and get to those who feel inferior, angry, and fearful about what was done to them. Ready, Set, Let's Go!

Credits

A SOUNDTRACK OF SCHIZOPHRENIA

Leona's Lyrics: The Sacrificial lamb

Editor/Proofreader: Reymani Mmr

Cover Designer: Reymani Mmr

Made in the USA
Columbia, SC
19 April 2021